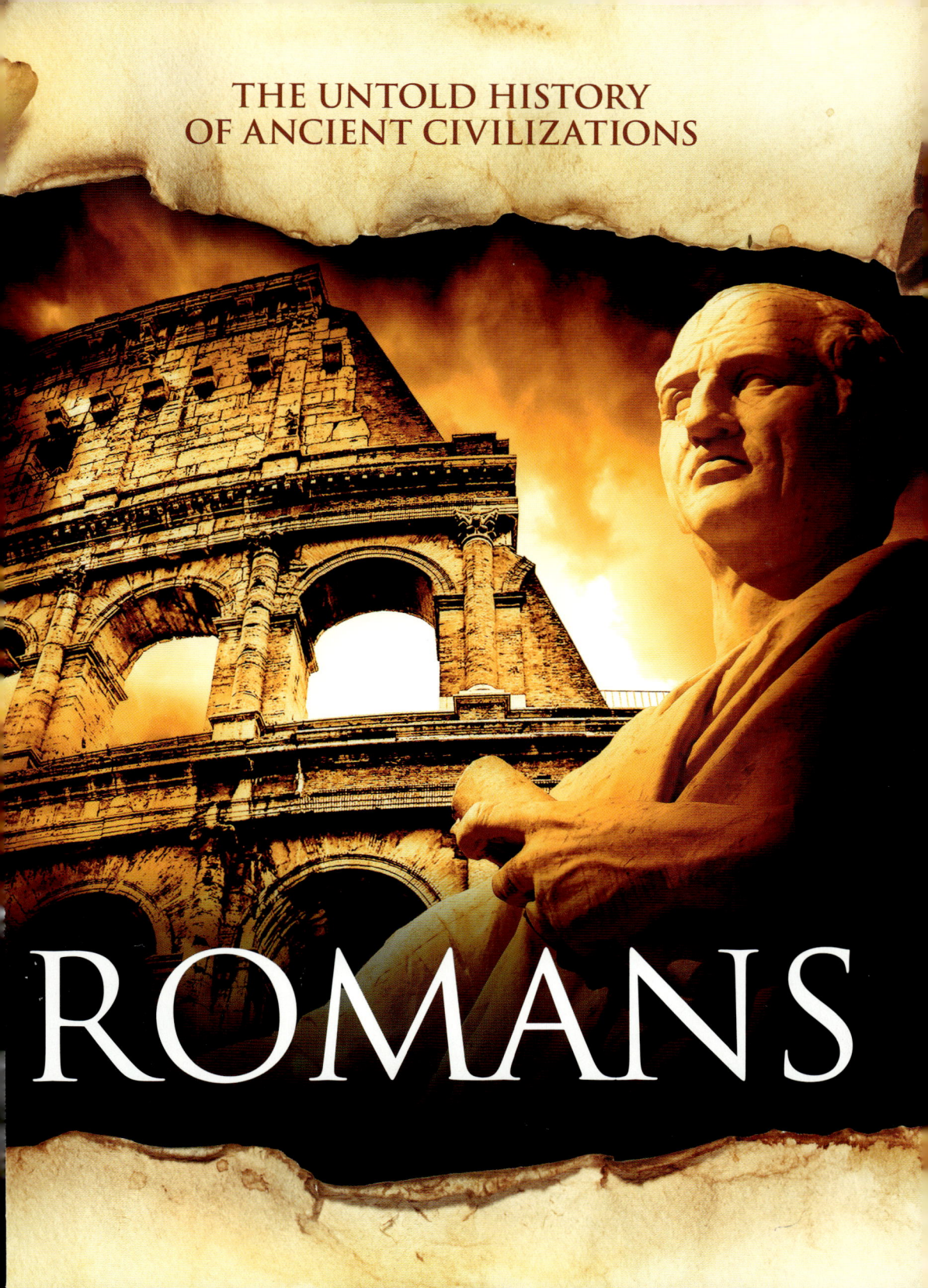

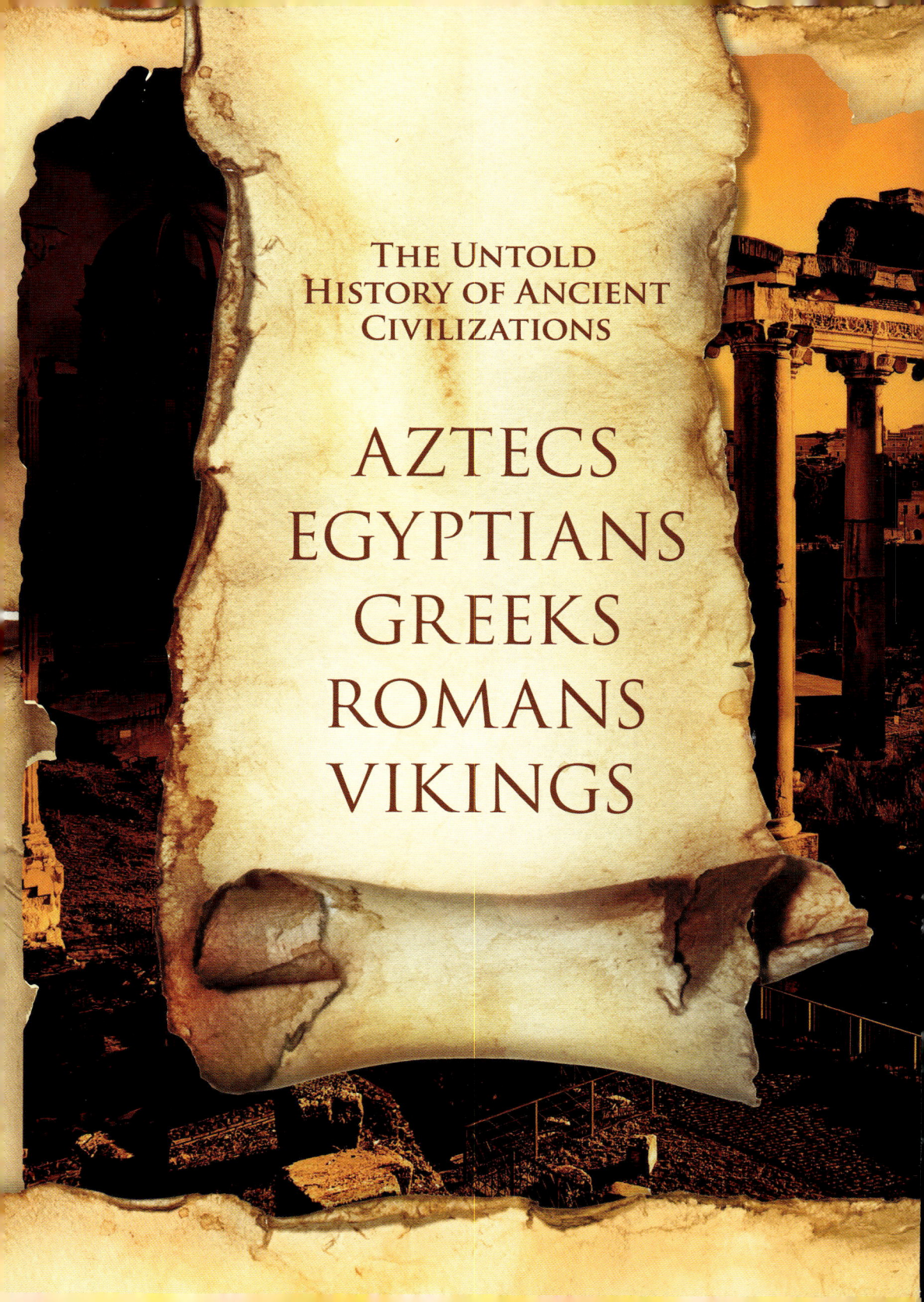

THE UNTOLD HISTORY
OF ANCIENT CIVILIZATIONS

ROMANS

MASON CREST
PHILADELPHIA
MIAMI

Mason Crest
450 Parkway Drive, Suite D
Broomall, Pennsylvania 19008
(866) MCP-BOOK (toll-free)
www.masoncrest.com

Copyright © 2019 by Mason Crest, an imprint of National Highlights, Inc. All rights reserved. No part of this publication may be reproduced or transmitted in any form or by any means, electronic or mechanical, including photocopying, recording, taping, or any information storage and retrieval system, without permission from the publisher.
First printing
9 8 7 6 5 4 3 2 1

ISBN (hardback) 978-1-4222-3521-8
ISBN (series) 978-1-4222-3517-1
ISBN (ebook) 978-1-4222-8341-7

Cataloging-in-Publication Data on file with the Library of Congress

Developed and produced by Mason Crest
Editor: Keri De Deo
Interior and cover design: Jana Rade
Production: Michelle Luke

QR CODES AND LINKS TO THIRD-PARTY CONTENT
You may gain access to certain third-party content ("Third-Party Sites") by scanning and using the QR Codes that appear in this publication (the "QR Codes"). We do not operate or control in any respect any information, products, or services on such Third-Party Sites linked to by us via the QR Codes included in this publication, and we assume no responsibility for any materials you may access using the QR Codes. Your use of the QR Codes may be subject to terms, limitations, or restrictions set forth in the applicable terms of use or otherwise established by the owners of the Third-Party Sites. Our linking to such Third-Party Sites via the QR Codes does not imply an endorsement or sponsorship of such Third-Party Sites or the information, products, or services offered on or through the Third-Party Sites, nor does it imply an endorsement or sponsorship of this publication by the owners of such Third-Party Sites.

CONTENTS

CHAPTER 1: THE PEOPLE WHO BUILT
    AN EMPIRE. 7
CHAPTER 2: WHO WANTS TO
    RULE THE WORLD? 11
CHAPTER 3: DREAM HOUSE. 15
CHAPTER 4: NO SUCH THING AS
    A SMALL FAMILY 19
CHAPTER 5: SERIOUS HIDE AND SEEK . 25
CHAPTER 6: FILL 'ER UP! 31
CHAPTER 7: ONE SIZE FITS ALL. 37
CHAPTER 8: EIGHT DAYS A WEEK. . . . 43
CHAPTER 9: BORROWED GODS 47
CHAPTER 10: A SOLDIER FOR LIFE . . . 51
CHAPTER 11: THE ROMAN
    FITNESS PROGRAM. . . . 55
ROMAN FACTS 58
FURTHER RESOURCES 60
INTERNET RESOURCES 61
EDUCATIONAL VIDEO LINKS
AND PHOTO CREDITS 62
INDEX. 63

KEY ICONS TO LOOK FOR:

WORDS TO UNDERSTAND: These words with their easy-to-understand definitions will increase the reader's understanding of the text while building vocabulary skills.

SIDEBARS: This boxed material within the main text allows readers to build knowledge, gain insights, explore possibilities, and broaden their perspectives by weaving together additional information to provide realistic and holistic perspectives.

EDUCATIONAL VIDEOS: Readers can view videos by scanning our QR codes, providing them with additional educational content to supplement the text. Examples include news coverage, moments in history, speeches, iconic sports moments, and much more!

TEXT-DEPENDENT QUESTIONS: These questions send the reader back to the text for more careful attention to the evidence presented there.

RESEARCH PROJECTS: Readers are pointed toward areas of further inquiry connected to each chapter. Suggestions are provided for projects that encourage deeper research and analysis.

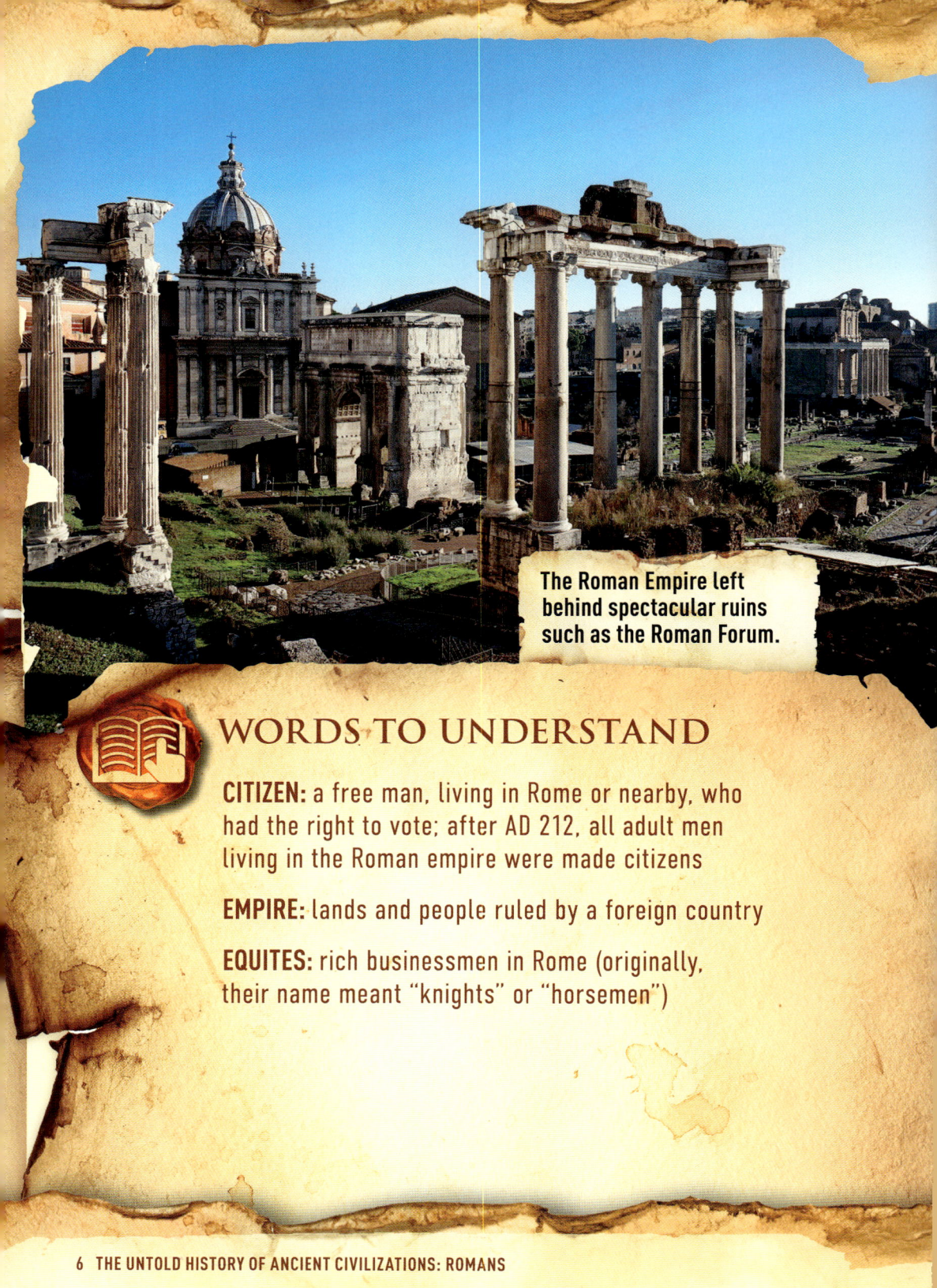

The Roman Empire left behind spectacular ruins such as the Roman Forum.

WORDS TO UNDERSTAND

CITIZEN: a free man, living in Rome or nearby, who had the right to vote; after AD 212, all adult men living in the Roman empire were made citizens

EMPIRE: lands and people ruled by a foreign country

EQUITES: rich businessmen in Rome (originally, their name meant "knights" or "horsemen")

CHAPTER 1

THE PEOPLE WHO BUILT AN EMPIRE

What words best describe the Romans? Conquerors? Yes. Artists? Yes. Statesmen? Absolutely. Just like people today, they were a mixture of nice and nasty, good and bad. They were brave, tough, hardworking, and devoted to duty. But they could also be cruel, bloodthirsty, greedy, and rude.

The Romans lived in Italy from about 753 BC to AD 476. They started with just one city, Rome. Over time, they took over surrounding lands. Between around 100 BC and AD 200, they built one of the greatest **empires** the world has seen.

Everyone living in Roman lands had to pay Roman taxes and obey Roman laws. But they were not all equal.

Learn about the rise of the Roman Empire in this video from the *National Geographic*.

CHAPTER 1: THE PEOPLE WHO BUILT AN EMPIRE 7

This map shows the extent of the Roman Empire at its most powerful in 117 AD.

A few *patricians* (nobles) and **equites** (businessmen) were rich. Most ordinary people, called *plebeians,* were poor. Roman **citizens**—a group of men who lived in and around Rome—could vote. Noncitizens had fewer rights. There was a class even below noncitizens—slaves. By law, slaves were like animals and could be beaten or starved by their owners.

TOO BIG TO FAIL?

The Romans had a favorite legend that described how their city began. It said that the very first Romans were twin boys, called Romulus and Remus. They were abandoned as babies and rescued by a friendly she-wolf. When the twins grew up, they decided to build a great human city. Romulus became king and named the city after himself.

Around AD 100, about 54 million men, women, and children were ruled by Rome. They included Celts, Germans, Greeks, Africans, Egyptians, and Jews. But it was hard to control and feed so many people. As the empire grew, it became harder and harder to defend the vast frontiers from invaders. In AD 476, the Roman government in Europe collapsed. Roman lands in the Middle East became part of a new Byzantine empire that lasted until 1453 BC.

Roman slaves helped build spectacular structures such as the Roman triumphal arch and amphitheater.

TEXT-DEPENDENT QUESTIONS

1. When did the Romans live in Italy?
2. Who does legend say first built the city of Rome?
3. When did the Roman Empire fall?

RESEARCH PROJECT

Research some of the items available in ancient Roman times that are not available today. What are some of the items we have today that didn't exist during ancient Roman times? Create a scavenger hunt for friends and family to follow where they collect items from either group. For example, avocadoes, potatoes, and bananas are food not available in Roman times, but they are widely available today. If you don't want to use the actual item, create drawings and hide them for people to find based on a poem or riddle.

CHAPTER 1: THE PEOPLE WHO BUILT AN EMPIRE 9

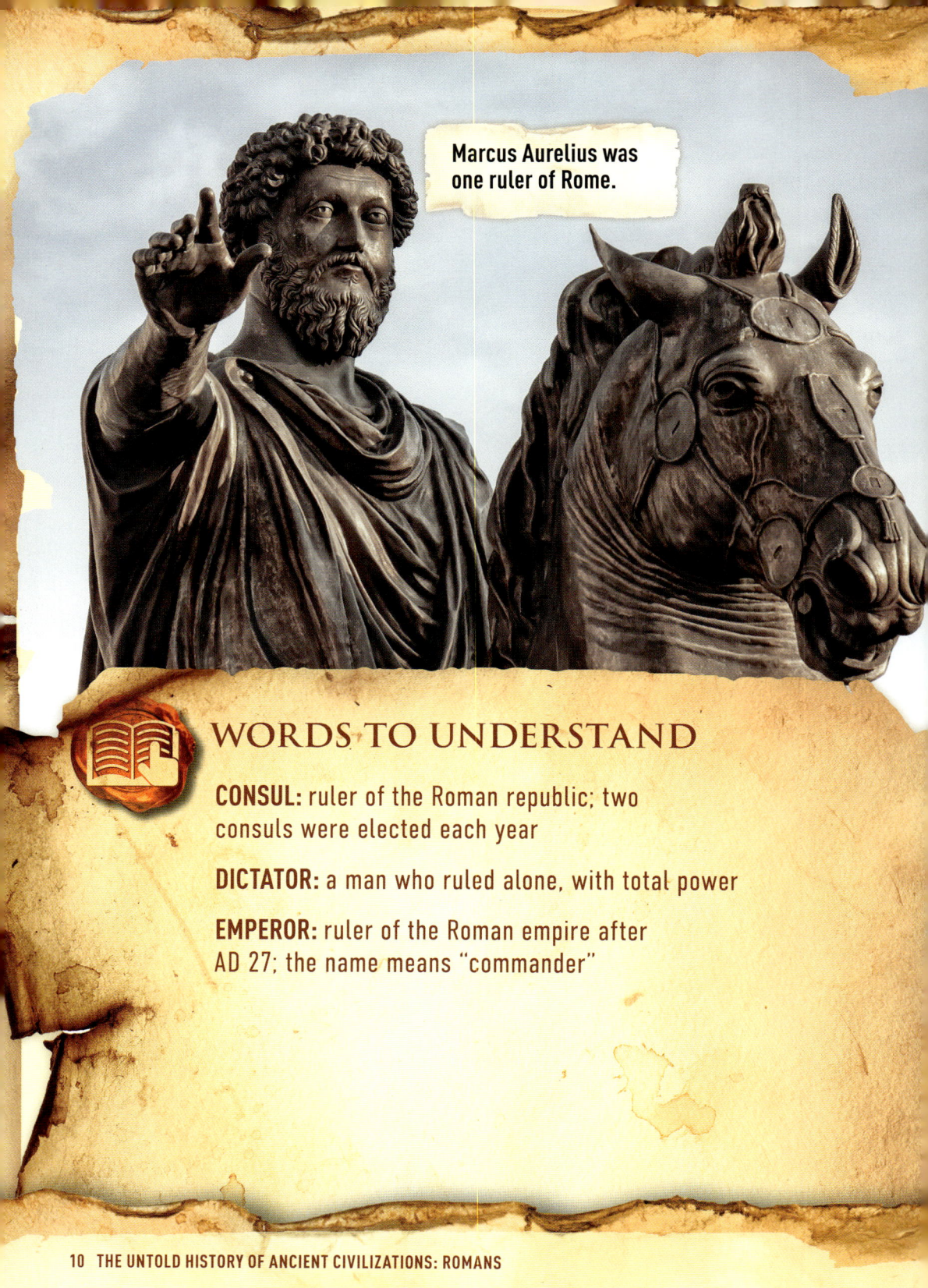

Marcus Aurelius was one ruler of Rome.

WORDS TO UNDERSTAND

CONSUL: ruler of the Roman republic; two consuls were elected each year

DICTATOR: a man who ruled alone, with total power

EMPEROR: ruler of the Roman empire after AD 27; the name means "commander"

CHAPTER 2

WHO WANTS TO RULE THE WORLD?

To rule Rome, to Romans, meant you ruled the world—and many wanted in on that job. Although at times Rome was a democracy of sorts, people did anything to gain power—bribes, frame-ups, even murder! Roman rulers were not squeamish when it came to violence.

At first, Rome was ruled by kings. The last was Tarquin the Proud. A better name might have been Tarquin the Cruel. On one occasion, he murdered a king and then had his wife ride over the body in a chariot. He also made false accusations against some senators so that he could steal their wealth and their lands. He tried to make Rome's citizens obey him by bullying and terrorizing them. Eventually, the people plotted to get rid of him, and he was thrown out in 509 BC.

RULERS WISE AND WICKED

Tarquin the Proud seized power after his brother's wife persuaded him to kill her father (who was king at the time), her husband (who was heir to the throne), and her sister (who was Tarquin's wife)! Once they were all dead, Tarquin became king. She then married him and became queen.

Rome then became a republic (a state ruled by the people). It had two leaders, called **consuls**. The Romans thought this was safer than letting one man rule alone. New consuls were chosen every year by the Senate, an assembly of rich, powerful men.

In wartime, the Senate could ask one man to become **dictator** for a while. But this was risky, both for the Senate and for the dictator. One brilliant army commander, Julius Caesar, took the position of **emperor** in 44 BC. He thought he had it all until he was stabbed to death by his comrades because they thought he was too fond of power.

One famous consul and orator was Cicero.

Julius Caesar was emperor in 44 BC.

> Augustus was the first emperor of ancient Rome.

After years of war and quarreling, Caesar's great-nephew, Augustus, became emperor of Rome. Many emperors ruled after him, until AD 476. Some were mad (like Caligula, who made his horse a consul), and some were bad (like Nero, suspected of burning down half of Rome). But others were wise and ruled well.

TEXT-DEPENDENT QUESTIONS

1. Who was the last king of Rome?
2. Why was Tarquin the Proud thrown out of power?
3. What happened to Julius Caesar?

RESEARCH PROJECT

The government of the United States is modeled after the Roman senate. Conduct some research to discover what other countries follow such a model. What's similar? What's different? Write a two- to three-page report. Ask your teacher if you can present this to your class.

CHAPTER 2: WHO WANTS TO RULE THE WORLD? 13

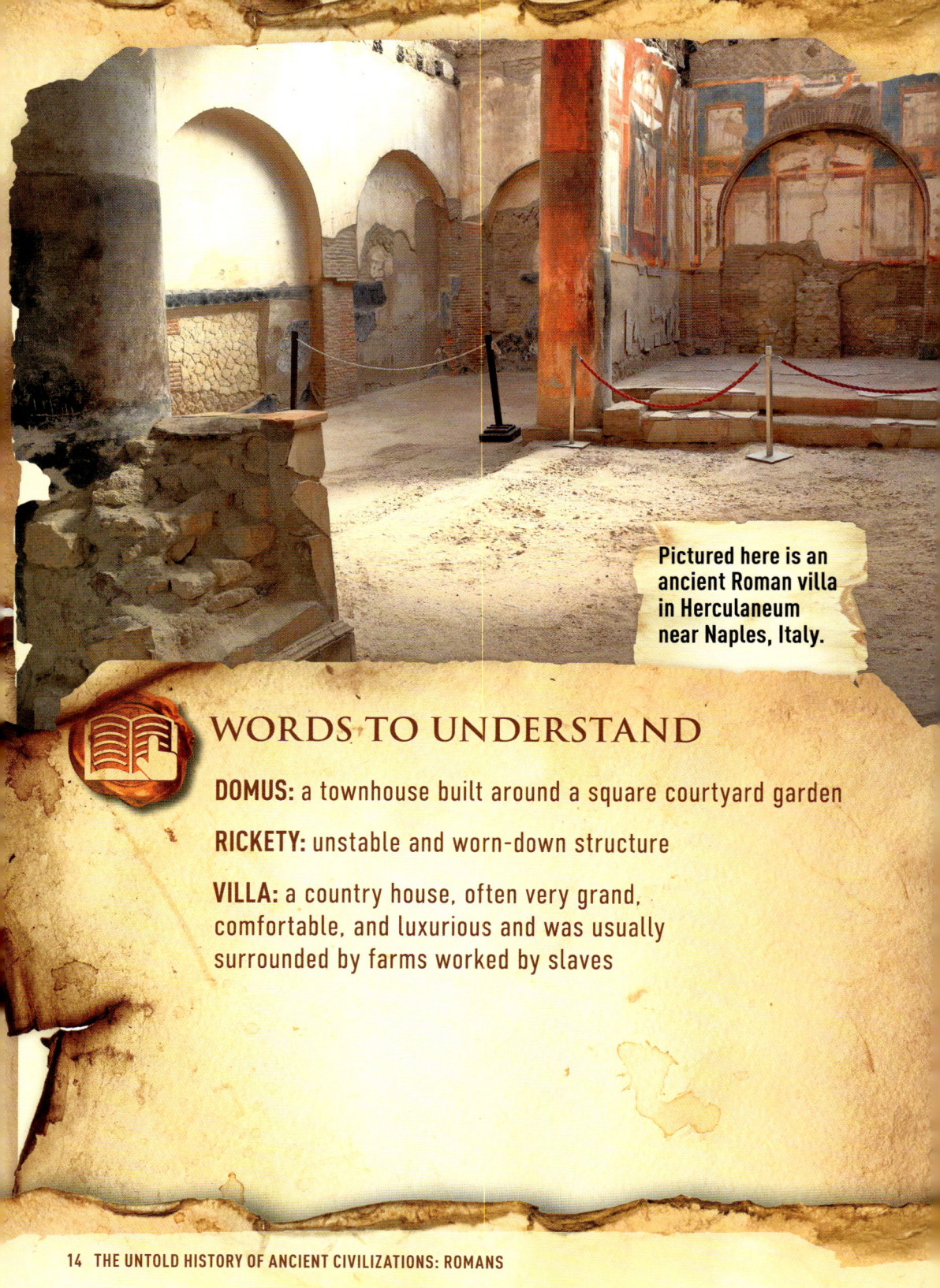

Pictured here is an ancient Roman villa in Herculaneum near Naples, Italy.

WORDS TO UNDERSTAND

DOMUS: a townhouse built around a square courtyard garden

RICKETY: unstable and worn-down structure

VILLA: a country house, often very grand, comfortable, and luxurious and was usually surrounded by farms worked by slaves

CHAPTER 3

DREAM HOUSE

Everyone has their idea of a dream house—perhaps a penthouse in a big city or a log cabin by a lake. Every Roman family dreamed of living in a **domus** or a **villa**. But, like today, not every Roman could afford such a home.

Columns like these were a part of most Roman buildings.

CHAPTER 3: DREAM HOUSE 15

Most people in the city rented cheap homes. Poor people in towns lived in small, cramped apartments, with just one or two rooms in **rickety** rows of buildings. In the country, poor families lived in wooden shacks with thatched roofs. They usually had small garden plots. They kept chickens or a pig and grew vegetables to support themselves.

Apartment buildings were known as *insulae* (islands). Each one was like a separate community. They had shops and

THE HOMELESS IN ROME

The homeless problem is as old as ancient Rome. Homeless Romans found shelter where they could, in the doorways of temples and law courts or under the covered walkways that surrounded city marketplaces. They kept a few belongings in baskets, which they chained to stone columns (part of all big Roman buildings), while they went to find food or have a wash at the public baths.

This ancient Rome street demonstrates the average ancient Roman insulae.

Many Roman buildings fell down or caught fire.

taverns on the ground floor and homeless people camping out on the roof! The best rooms were on the first floor. They had windows, which let in light and air, and balconies. The worst rooms were in the attic. These were dark, stuffy, and damp.

There were no building codes in ancient Rome. Insulae were usually very badly built of timber and sun-dried mud. They often fell down. They caught fire, too, because Roman people liked to keep warm by huddling round clay pots full of burning coals. Emperor Augustus tried to make blocks safer by limiting their height to 63 feet (21 m). He also set up a fire brigade run by slaves, but many people still died, trapped under rubble or in flames.

TEXT-DEPENDENT QUESTIONS

1. What kind of home did the Roman rich live in?
2. Why were insulae dangerous?
3. What did Emperor Augustus do to try to make the insulae safer?

RESEARCH PROJECT

Class distinctions between the poor and the rich exist all over the world. Where do some of the poorest people live? What can be done to help them? Write a two- to three-page report discussing ways to help the world's poor people.

CHAPTER 3: DREAM HOUSE 17

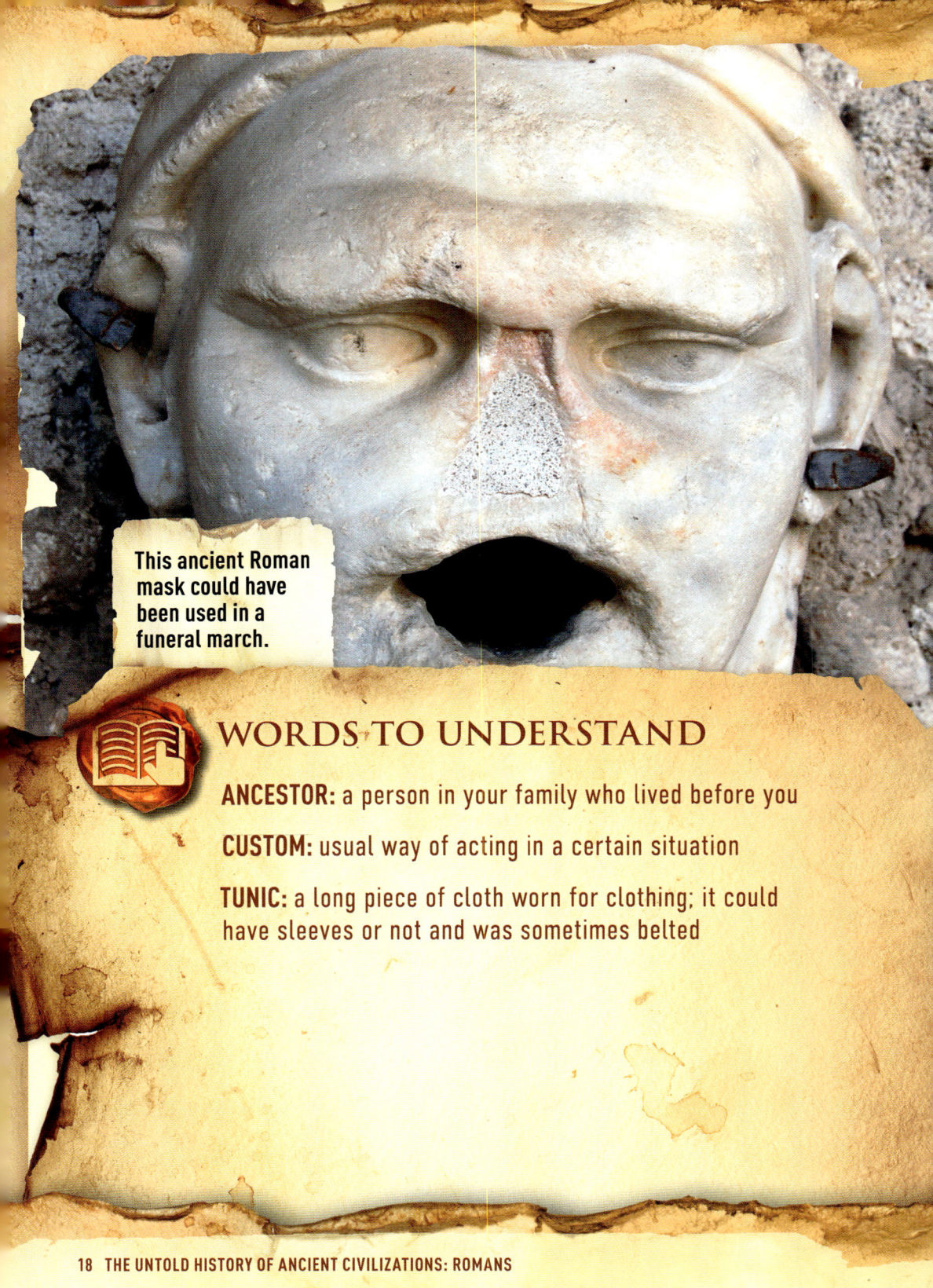

This ancient Roman mask could have been used in a funeral march.

WORDS TO UNDERSTAND

ANCESTOR: a person in your family who lived before you

CUSTOM: usual way of acting in a certain situation

TUNIC: a long piece of cloth worn for clothing; it could have sleeves or not and was sometimes belted

CHAPTER 4

NO SUCH THING AS A SMALL FAMILY

Everyone who lived in your house was part of your family. So, your parents, brothers and sisters, grandparents, aunts, uncles, cousins—and even slaves—all belong to your family unit. Each family also had its own guardian spirits and **ancestor** gods, called *lares* and *genii*. Romans were proud of their ancestors. They made wax masks of their faces after they died and displayed them like photos. The head of each family was the oldest living man, or *paterfamilias*. He was like a little emperor. He had the power of life and death over the whole family, including his wife. All family members had to obey him and honor him (and the spirits of dead ancestors who lived in him) with prayers on his birthday.

Do you wonder what it would be like living in ancient Rome? This video gives you a good idea of what it was like in a Roman family.

CHAPTER 4: NO SUCH THING AS A SMALL FAMILY 19

Ancient Roman women were not seen as equal to men.

A WEDDING TO REMEMBER

Divorce was quite common in Roman times. Usually, a couple decided to end a marriage. Sometimes families caused divorces for political reasons. Cato was a famous Roman politician. His friend Hortensius wanted to marry a member of Cato's family to show his support. So Hortensius asked Cato to divorce his own wife, so he could marry her instead. Amazingly, Cato agreed.

Girls could marry when they were twelve years old; most men waited until they were around twenty. Just like is common today, weddings were held in June, and Roman wedding **customs** stayed the same for hundreds of years. The bride's hair was arranged with a sharp-pointed spear! And she was dressed in a white wool **tunic** with a yellow cloak and flame-colored veil and shoes.

Wedding guests came to her family home for a feast. The bride and groom linked hands, shared food, and threw walnuts as a sign of leaving childhood

20 THE UNTOLD HISTORY OF ANCIENT CIVILIZATIONS: ROMANS

Much like today, ancient Roman weddings held important cultural traditions.

behind. Then the groom would carry the bride over the doorstep. He wanted to prevent her from stumbling or falling as she entered her new home, which Romans thought would bring lifelong bad luck! Once inside, he presented her with a key to the house along with water and fire.

The ancient Roman tradition of carrying a bride over the threshold is still practiced today.

Braided hair was a popular ancient Roman wedding style.

TEXT-DEPENDENT QUESTIONS

1. What did the ancient Romans do to honor their dead ancestors?
2. When were weddings most commonly held?
3. Why did a Roman groom carry his bride over the doorstep?

RESEARCH PROJECT

Some of the ancient Roman wedding rituals are similar to other cultural wedding rituals. This site, https://www.explore-italian-culture.com/ancient-roman-fashion.html, explains some of the traditions involved in an ancient Roman wedding. One such fashion was a Roman braid called the tutulus. Conduct a research for videos on this ancient Roman trend, and practice making similar braids. You can practice on yarn, embroidery floss, or string.

CHAPTER 4: NO SUCH THING AS A SMALL FAMILY

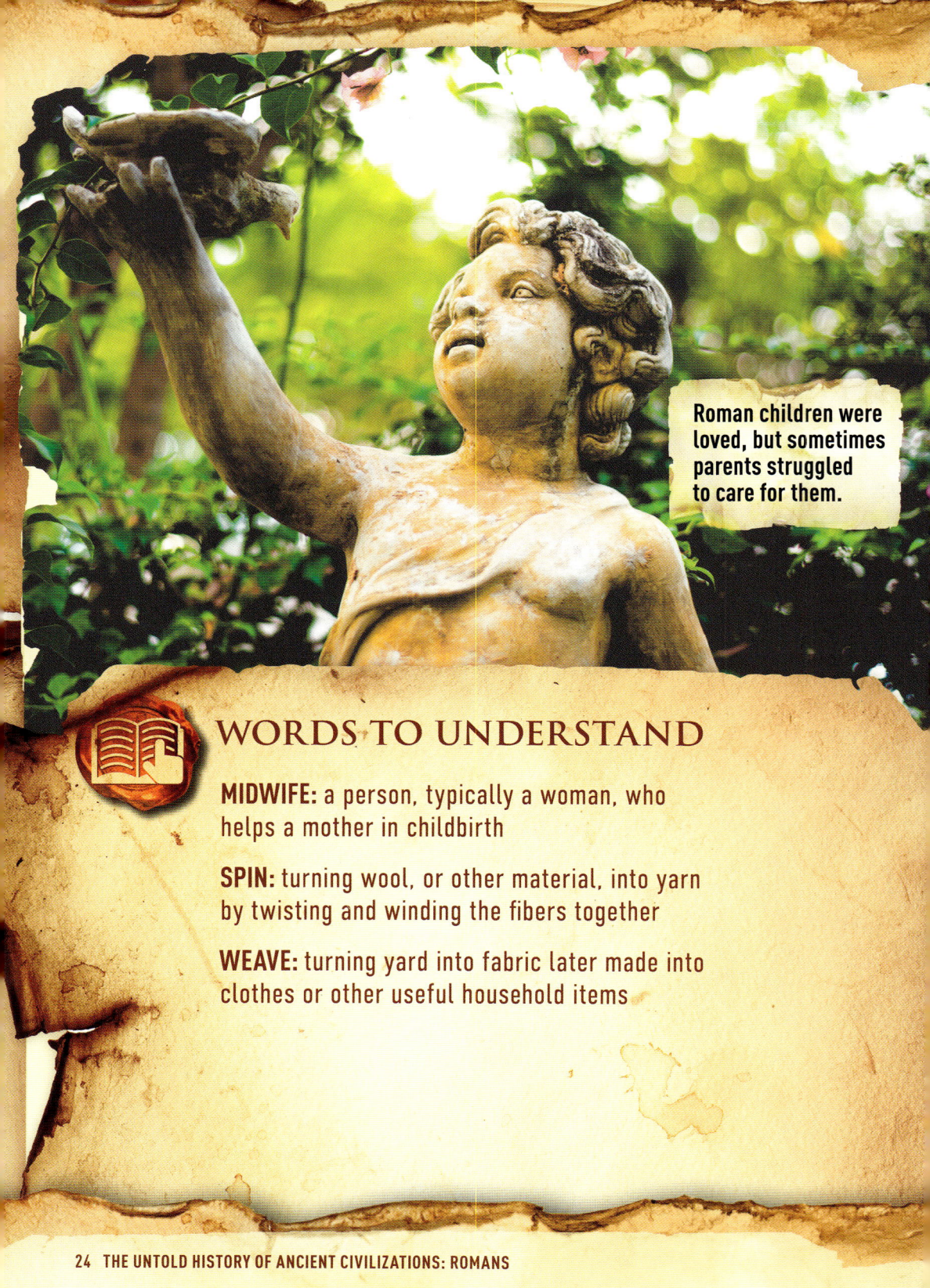

Roman children were loved, but sometimes parents struggled to care for them.

WORDS TO UNDERSTAND

MIDWIFE: a person, typically a woman, who helps a mother in childbirth

SPIN: turning wool, or other material, into yarn by twisting and winding the fibers together

WEAVE: turning yard into fabric later made into clothes or other useful household items

CHAPTER 5

SERIOUS HIDE AND SEEK

In Roman times, kids who wished for baby brothers or sisters were often disappointed. Most Roman parents loved their children, but they didn't want many of them. Poor parents could not afford to feed lots of children. And rich families did not want to divide their money in so many ways.

Children born to rich families did not always have an easy life.

A father decided whether babies born in his house should survive. A **midwife** laid each new baby at his feet. If he picked it up, it was welcomed into the family. If he did not, it was left outside on a manure heap. Childless women or slave traders would visit the dumps every day, hoping to find a baby to adopt or to raise and sell.

FIRST NAME'S FIRST

Roman girls were named on the eighth day after birth and boys one day later. Boys had two names, a personal one and a family one. Some had nicknames, too. But girls were just called by the female version of their family name. This meant that sisters' names were all the same. To avoid confusion, parents gave their daughters numbers—Prima (first), Secunda (Second), Tertia (Third), and so on.

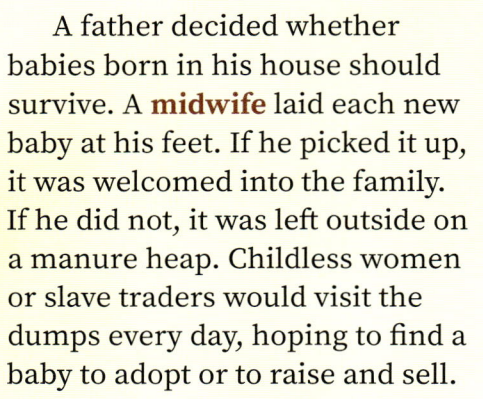

These ruins are of Colosseum of Capua, a gladiator school.

Ancient Roman girls were taught to weave.

Rich boys went to school, where they learned reading, writing, math, and public speaking. Going to school had high stakes—a wrong answer would mean getting hit with a stick. Rich girls had lessons at home. They learned reading, writing, music, and how to keep accounts and manage slaves. Although many families bought clothes from craft workshops, girls also were taught how to **spin** and **weave**. Even Emperor Augustus, the richest man in the world, insisted that his daughter weave all his clothes.

Ancient Roman writing tablets were made from wood and wax.

Poor boys and girls did not go to school. They had to work as soon as they were able, fetching water, running errands, looking after younger brothers and sisters, or helping their parents in shops, in workshops, and on farms.

TEXT-DEPENDENT QUESTIONS

1. How old was a girl before she was named?
2. What did rich boys study in school?
3. What were girls taught?

RESEARCH PROJECT

MAKE A ROMAN WRITING TABLET

Romans wrote letters and stories on long parchment scrolls. But they used little writing tablets, made of wood covered with wax, to make quick notes and rough jottings. They wrote on the wax with a stick called a stylus. One end was pointed for making marks in the wax. The other end was rounded for smoothing out mistakes.

YOU WILL NEED:
- A small, shallow box with a lid
- Sticky tape
- Heavy-duty sticky modeling clay (plasticine)
- An empty ballpoint pen
- A rolling pin

INSTRUCTIONS:

1. Stick the bottom and the lid of the box together with tape along one of the long sides.

2. Roll out the modeling clay to fit neatly inside the box lid and bottom. It should be at least ½ inch (1 cm) thick.

3. Use the empty ballpoint to write in the modelling clay. Try writing some Roman words, such as puer (boy), puella (girl), mater (mother), pater (father), magister (teacher), amicus (male friend), or amica (female friend).

Barley porridge was a staple in ancient Roman cooking.

WORDS TO UNDERSTAND

GARLAND: a wreath of flowers worn like jewelry or hung as decoration around the house

PORRIDGE: a food boiled to a thick consistency in water or milk; much like modern-day oatmeal

VAST: a large amount or size; enormous

CHAPTER 6

FILL 'ER UP!

What would it be like having one hot meal a day? No matter how wealthy, that's what most Romans did. Because they had no kitchens in their homes (or refrigerators, either), ordinary families went to shops and markets for takeout food! Country people cooked their meals over an open fire, usually something like barley **porridge**.

For breakfast, ancient Romans ate bread dipped in liquid.

The Roman empire was huge, and food varied from place to place. But generally, for breakfast, nearly everyone ate bread dipped in water, vinegar, or diluted wine. For lunch, there was more bread, with a little cheese, olive oil, cold meat, or fruit. Figs and grapes, eaten fresh or dried, were the cheapest, most plentiful fruits, but the Romans also enjoyed apples, pears, mulberries, and dates.

STUFFED TO THE GILLS

During a feast, guests were entertained with music, singing and dancing, or poetry readings. They were encouraged to keep on eating, even if they were so full it made them sick. Some guests carried a feather with them to tickle their own throats and make themselves vomit more quickly.

Lentils with spices and garlic were common food for ancient Romans.

The main meal of the day was *cena* (dinner), eaten late in the afternoon. Roman gardeners grew beans, lentils, beetroot, lettuce, cabbage, radishes, and lots of onions and garlic. Everything was seasoned with the Romans' favorite sauce, called *garum*. It was made from fish innards, left for months to rot in the sun.

For rich families, dinner was a chance to display their wealth and impress important guests. They paid **vast** sums to skilled chefs to create sumptuous feasts. The ideal number of diners was nine. They stretched out on three couches, arranged around a low table. Slaves washed the guests' hands and feet and gave them

The Roman palette enjoyed a variety of foods.

CHAPTER 6: FILL 'ER UP! 33

garlands of flowers to wear. Dinner party food was often very strange. Some of the food offered was even forbidden. Romans liked soft, fatty meats, such as calves' brain, or sows' udders, or milk-fed mice and snails. They enjoyed strong, spicy flavors and foods in disguise—such as roast hare dressed up to look like a flying horse.

This carrot recipe makes an excellent side dish for any entree

TEXT-DEPENDENT QUESTIONS

1. What was the typical ancient Roman breakfast?
2. What was the main meal of the day called?
3. What was the Roman's favorite sauce made from?

RESEARCH PROJECT

MAKE CARROTS IN SWEET-SOUR SAUCE

You will need:

- 2 cups (500 g) cut carrots
- 3 tsp. (15 ml) cooking oil
- 1 tsp. (5 ml) ground cumin
- 1 tsp. (5 ml) ground coriander
- 3 tsp. (15 ml) honey OR brown sugar
- 3 tsp. (15 ml) water
- 3 tsp. (15 ml) vinegar
- 3 tsp. (15 ml) currants, raisins, or sultanas (optional)
- 1 tsp. (5 ml) Thai fish sauce (tastes rather like Roman garum) OR good pinch each of salt and pepper
- 3 tsp. (15 ml) chopped fresh parsley OR 1 tsp. (5 ml) dried parsley
- 1 tsp. (5 ml) corn flour or maize starch plus 3 tsp. (15 ml) water

Ask an adult to help you.

1. Put carrots in a saucepan with a lid. Add just enough water to cover them.
2. Boil carrots until tender (5–10 minutes).
3. To make the sauce, put oil, cumin, and coriander into a separate small pan. Mix well, heat, and let bubble for 2 or 3 minutes. Do not let the mixture burn.
4. Add honey OR sugar and water and vinegar to the oil and spices in a small pan. Stir well. Heat gently, and keep on stirring until the honey or sugar is dissolved.
5. Carefully bring sauce mixture to the boil. Let it bubble for 2 or 3 minutes, stirring all the time. Turn down the heat, and add Thai fish sauce OR salt and pepper, plus fresh OR dried parsley, and currants, raisins, or sultanas, if using.
6. Bring to a boil again, then pour the sauce mixture over the carrots and their cooking water.
7. Mix cornflour with water. Add to the carrots and sauce. Mix very well, then heat gently to boiling point, stirring all the time. Serve.

This Roman statue of an orator (speaker) holding a scroll demonstrates clearly what the Romans wore.

WORDS TO UNDERSTAND

FRILL: a strip of cloth or lace worn at the edge of a garment; ruffle

PALLA: cloak or shawl worn by Roman women

STOLA: a floor-length over-tunic, worn by women

CHAPTER 7

ONE SIZE FITS ALL

Imagine using a beach towel as your everyday clothes. The Romans used just one long rectangle of cloth wrapped around their bodies for clothes. One form was a *toga* (a cloak for men), another a **stola** (a trailing over-tunic, for women), and a third was a **palla** (big shawl). Not everyone looked the same, though. They held the cloth in place with different belts, brooches, and pins. Poor people used the same pieces of cloth as blankets at night.

Roman fashions changed over the years, especially for men. At first, all men wore togas (usually with nothing underneath). Then Greek-style tunics became popular, although priests, senators, and lawyers still had togas for special occasions. Tunics were simpler to put on than togas and much easier to move in. To keep warm, men wore cloaks of wool or leather, sometimes with a hood or several tunics on top of each other.

Watch this video to learn how to make your own Roman toga.

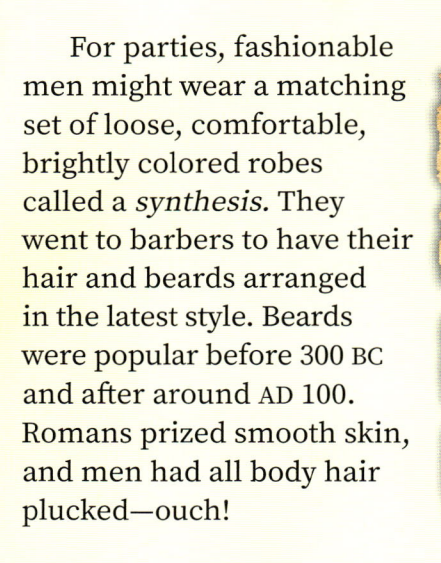

For parties, fashionable men might wear a matching set of loose, comfortable, brightly colored robes called a *synthesis*. They went to barbers to have their hair and beards arranged in the latest style. Beards were popular before 300 BC and after around AD 100. Romans prized smooth skin, and men had all body hair plucked—ouch!

THE PRICE OF BEAUTY

Many Roman women—and some men— wore cosmetics made from powdered chalk, lead, lichen, stale wine, and ashes. They cared for their skin with olive oil, milk, and ointments—made of bird droppings. Often, these mixtures did more harm than good. Some were really poisonous—so much so that they could keep your brain from working right.

Some Roman men wore beards.

Roman women's clothes were similar to men's but longer. Women and girls wore an ankle-length tunic with a stola on top and draped a palla around their shoulders. In company, many married women also covered their hair. Rich women's clothes often had colored borders and could be trimmed with **frills** at the hem. Underneath, many women wore a wide band of soft cloth around the upper body, like a bra. For playing sports, women might wear something like a modern bikini.

At a festival in England, these women model a modern interpretation of ancient Roman dress.

This statue of Minerva, goddess of Rome, shows how women dressed at the time.

CHAPTER 7: ONE SIZE FITS ALL 39

This illustration provides a vision of what ancient Romans wore.

40 THE UNTOLD HISTORY OF ANCIENT CIVILIZATIONS: ROMANS

TEXT-DEPENDENT QUESTIONS

1. What is a toga?
2. What was a brightly colored robe called?
3. How did Roman men and women dress differently?

RESEARCH PROJECT

Make a Roman Toga

You will need:

- King-size white pillowcase
- ¼ yard (22.86 cm) thin fabric the color of your choice for sash
- 1 yard (91.44 cm) gold cording or rope
- Fray check (if using natural-fabric pillowcase)
- Scissors
- Iron

Instructions.

1. Turn pillowcase inside out, and then cut lines at the top for the head and on the side for arms.
2. Next, seal cut edges of fabric to avoid fraying.
3. Turn pillowcase right side out and iron.
4. Drape the colored fabric over one shoulder for a sash, and tie the gold cording or rope around the waist to secure.
5. If needed, glue the gold cording or rope to the fabric so it will hold more securely.

Adapted from hgtv.com

Roman baths were a popular holiday spot.

WORDS TO UNDERSTAND

CIRCUS: oval track, surrounded by seats, used for chariot races

GLADIATOR: slave, criminal, or (occasionally) volunteer who fought to entertain the public

JAVELIN: a spear, often made of wood, that is thrown by hand for sport

CHAPTER 8

EIGHT DAYS A WEEK

Everyone loves a holiday. Many Roman children had every eighth day off of school for market day. Adults had the day off, too, and law courts and government offices were closed. On that day, men and women dressed in their best and set out to do their shopping, visit their friends, play games, or watch sports.

There were also many religious holidays throughout the year. Some lasted for almost a week. To relax at holiday times, Romans went to the baths, sports centers, and theaters. They watched dancers, mime shows, and acrobats, listened to music and poetry, or walked and talked with friends.

Young men played team games similar to hockey and volleyball, lifted weights, rowed, ran races, threw the discus and **javelin**, boxed, wrestled, and went swimming. Less active games, played by women as well as men, included draughts, dice, and *tall* (like jacks played with the anklebones of sheep and goats). They even played tic-tac-toe.

A FREE AFTERNOON

Romans began work very early in the morning and completed their tasks by midafternoon. They then took a short siesta (daytime sleep) and were free to enjoy the rest of the day.

The most exciting Roman entertainment was chariot racing and **gladiator** fights. They were also the most dangerous. The biggest sports stadium was the Circus Maximus, with seats for 250,000 people. At the **Circus**, daring charioteers drove teams of horses seven times round a narrow course—a total distance of about 5 miles (8 km). There were often crashes, when chariots overturned and horses and drivers were killed. Charioteers wore knives so that, if they were thrown from their chariots, they could cut themselves free before being dragged or trampled.

These reconstructed weapons are similar to ancient Roman javelins.

This is what's left of the Circus Maximus.

44 THE UNTOLD HISTORY OF ANCIENT CIVILIZATIONS: ROMANS

Gladiator fights were even more violent. Romans liked to see men fight and watch animals being killed for fun. Politicians and other powerful people sponsored shows and handed out free tickets, hoping the citizens would support them in return. Gladiators, who were usually slaves, prisoners of war, or criminals, were treated like glamorous superstars. Even a few women became famous gladiators before they were banned around AD 200. But their lives were short.

Gladiators often fought to the death.

TEXT-DEPENDENT QUESTIONS

1. What games did the children play on their days off?
2. What did the Romans do for entertainment?
3. Describe a gladiator's life.

RESEARCH PROJECT

Conduct some research on the Internet to find descriptions of ancient Roman toys and games. How were these toys and games different from modern games or toys? Create a video or picture presentation demonstrating some of the similarities between the ancient and modern games.

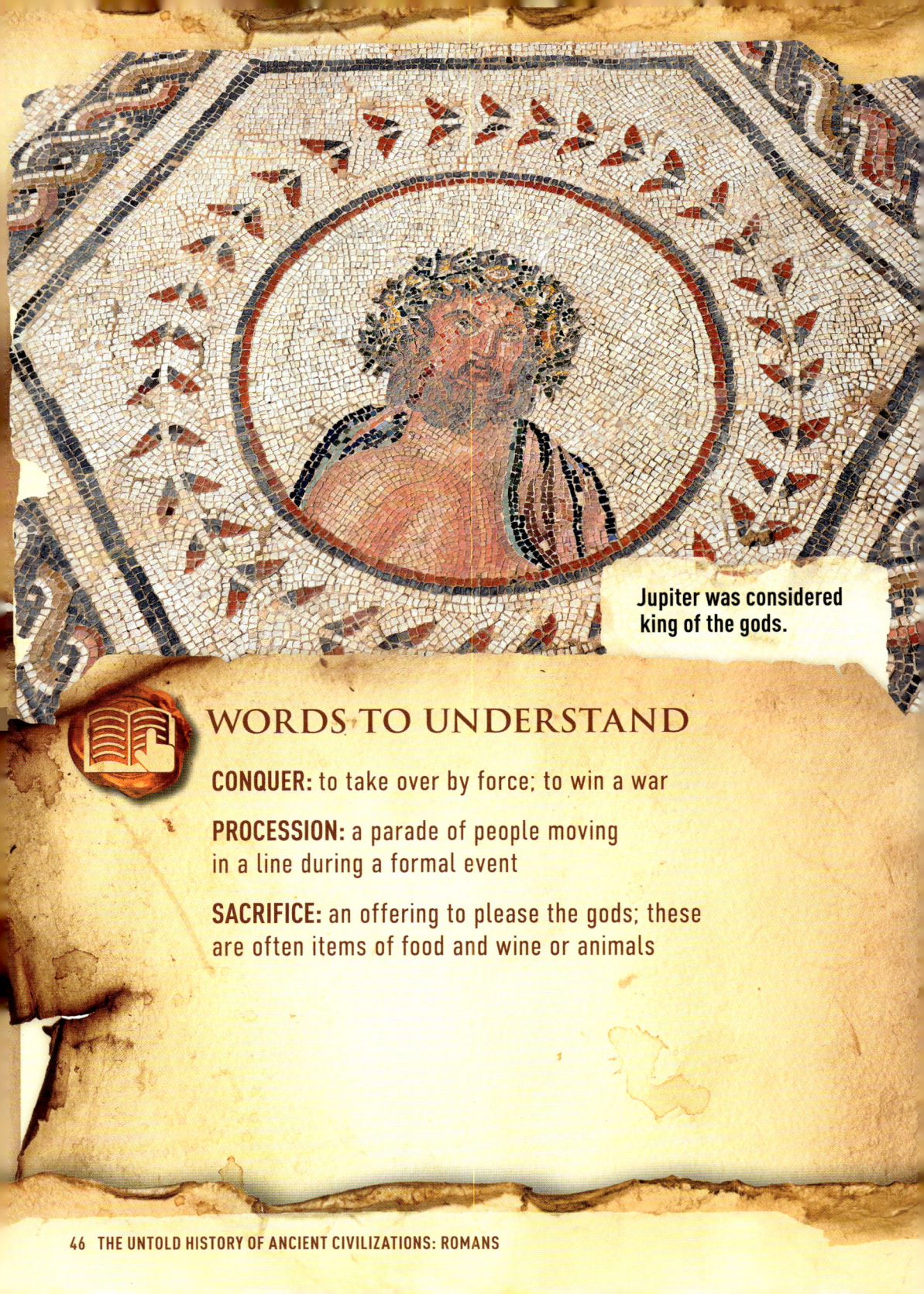

Jupiter was considered king of the gods.

WORDS TO UNDERSTAND

CONQUER: to take over by force; to win a war

PROCESSION: a parade of people moving in a line during a formal event

SACRIFICE: an offering to please the gods; these are often items of food and wine or animals

CHAPTER 9

BORROWED GODS

Romans **conquered** many kinds of people—and they borrowed some of their customs and traditions, including the gods and goddesses they worshipped. Some came from the Greeks, but the Romans changed their names to sound more Roman. Others were old Italian gods or spirits who were thought to live in caves, rivers, and trees. Romans often chose which gods to make their own, but everyone had to honor the spirits of dead and living emperors.

Jupiter was the most important. He was god of the sky and protector of the Roman state. Mars was the god of war, Venus was the goddess of love, and Vesta was the goddess of fire. All the gods were served by priests and priestesses.

Mars was the Roman god of war.

CHAPTER 9: BORROWED GODS 47

Roman people also looked for messages sent by the gods, especially before starting something important, like setting off on a journey, making a business deal, or declaring war. Messages could be read in the weather, in mysterious events like eclipses, and in animals.

Janus was the god of the new year.

Public prayers, **sacrifices**, and **processions** were very important. They helped the Romans please the gods and ask for their help. But if anything went wrong, like a priest sneezing, then the ritual would be worthless. So, the Romans rarely tried rituals very close to important events.

ROMAN GOD ROLL CALL

The Romans worshipped many gods and goddesses. Here are some of them:

Jupiter—king of the gods
Juno—queen of the gods
Mars—god of war
Venus—goddess of love
Minerva—goddess of wisdom
Diana—goddess of hunting and the moon
Neptune—god of the sea
Mercury—messenger of the gods
Pluto—god of the underworld
Vesta—goddess of fire and the hearth
Vulcan—god of fire and volcanoes
Janus—god of doorways, beginnings, and the new year

The Roman year was full of religious festivals. Work and government business were not allowed. Most festivals were full of fun, such as *Saturnalia,* in midwinter, when people gave presents, wore funny hats, and played gambling games.

New gods and strange ceremonies came to Rome from conquered lands. Soldiers worshipped the Persian god Mithras, with bull's blood, deep underground. Priests of the Syrian goddess Cybele whipped themselves into a frenzy and danced through the streets.

This statue of Mithras at the underground Mithraeum temple in the ancient Roman town of Osta Antica.

TEXT-DEPENDENT QUESTIONS

1. According to the Romans, who was the most important god?
2. When was the *Saturnalia* festival celebrated?
3. What god did soldiers worship?

RESEARCH PROJECT

Many of the Roman gods are the same as the Greek gods—they just have different names. Create a side-by-side chart of the Roman and Greek gods. Which ones are the same? Which ones are different? Find images of these gods, and create a photo collage of the Roman and Greek gods.

CHAPTER 9: BORROWED GODS

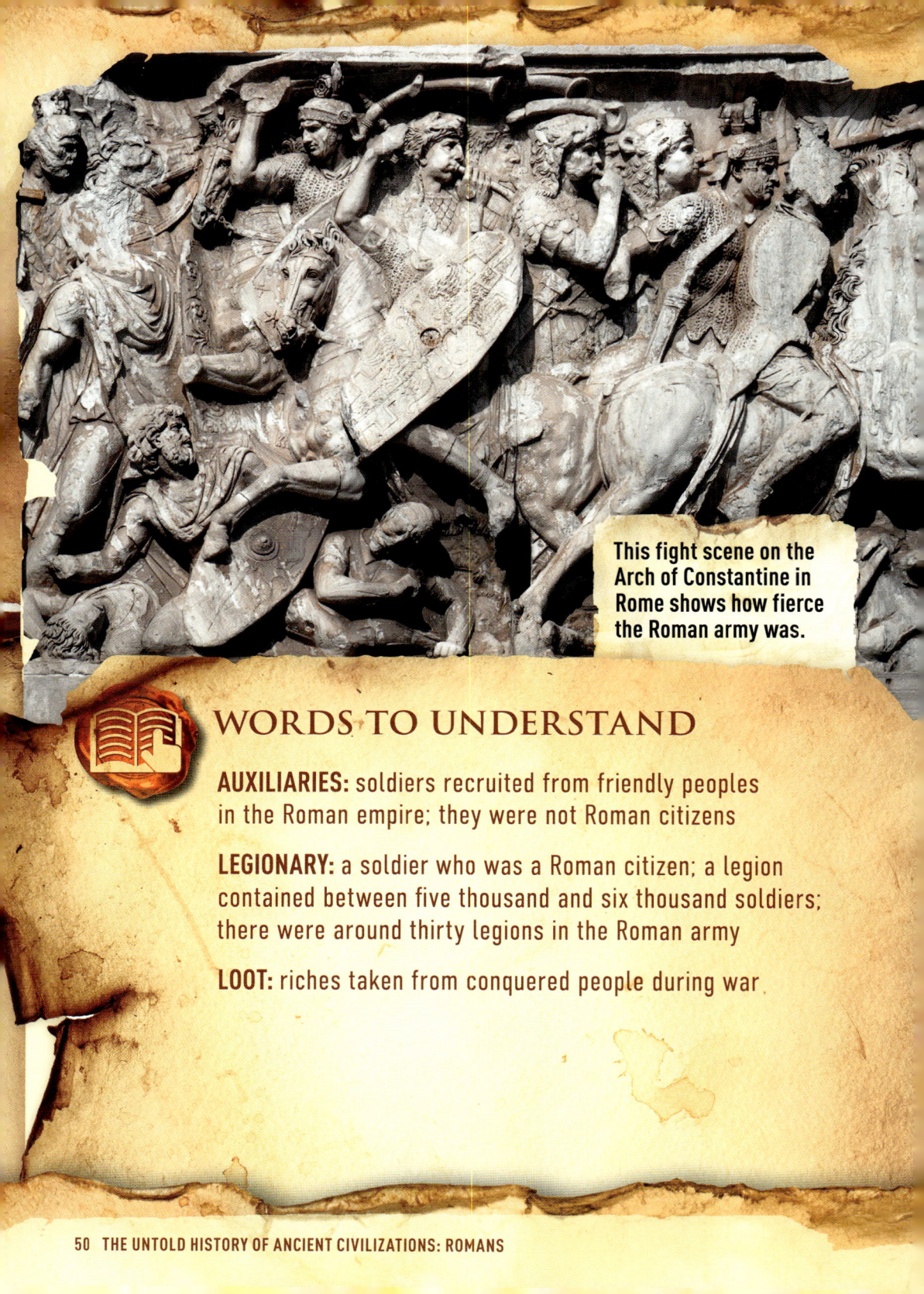

This fight scene on the Arch of Constantine in Rome shows how fierce the Roman army was.

WORDS TO UNDERSTAND

AUXILIARIES: soldiers recruited from friendly peoples in the Roman empire; they were not Roman citizens

LEGIONARY: a soldier who was a Roman citizen; a legion contained between five thousand and six thousand soldiers; there were around thirty legions in the Roman army

LOOT: riches taken from conquered people during war

CHAPTER 10

A SOLDIER FOR LIFE

During their time, no one was more feared than the Roman army. They conquered and made Rome into the superpower. But Roman soldiers didn't just fight. They built splendid roads, walls, forts, and camps. They spread Roman words, ideas, beliefs, and customs wherever they went.

The Roman army was big, fit, well trained, and disciplined. Between AD 100 and 200, when the empire was most powerful, it contained more than 150,000 **legionaries** and even more **auxiliaries**. Soldiers signed on for almost all their active adult life: legionaries had to serve for twenty years, auxiliaries for twenty-five years. Because they were gone so long, Roman soldiers got lonely, and their mothers would send them care packages. They were well paid, but each man had to buy his own food.

A SOLDIER'S WORKOUT

Each soldier had to march carrying his weapons, armor, helmet, shield, cloak, leather bottle (for water or wine), cooking pot, metal dish, spade and mattock (for digging defensive ditches), first aid kit, and two weeks' food. All this weighed more than 90 pounds (40 kg).

A Roman's uniform and equipment weighed more than 90 pounds (40 kg).

Soldiers kept themselves fit and ready for battle by going on long, 20-mile (30-km) marches each day, practicing with their weapons, and playing sports. They needed to be tough to survive a battle. Soldiers who fought bravely were rewarded with crowns of oak leaves or plaited grass—but they also hoped to get a share of **loot** from conquered enemies. A bold, lucky fighter might make his fortune this way.

Officers kept their men in line through strict discipline. At best, a soldier who made a mistake would have his rations or pay reduced, or he might be whipped. Men who ran away or disobeyed orders were killed. One commander even executed his own son. Savage punishments like "decimation" forced soldiers to behave. If just one man in a cohort (unit of 500 soldiers) broke the rules, one in every ten was killed, even though most of them had done nothing wrong. The men to die were chosen by lot.

Several stone carvings of the Roman army exist.

TEXT-DEPENDENT QUESTIONS

1. Besides fighting, what were the duties of a Roman soldier?
2. How long did a Roman soldier have to serve?
3. What happened to a Roman soldier who disobeyed orders?

RESEARCH PROJECT

Looking at some of the images from this chapter, and conducting a web search, recreate some of the soldier uniforms of the ancient Romans.

CHAPTER 10: A SOLDIER FOR LIFE

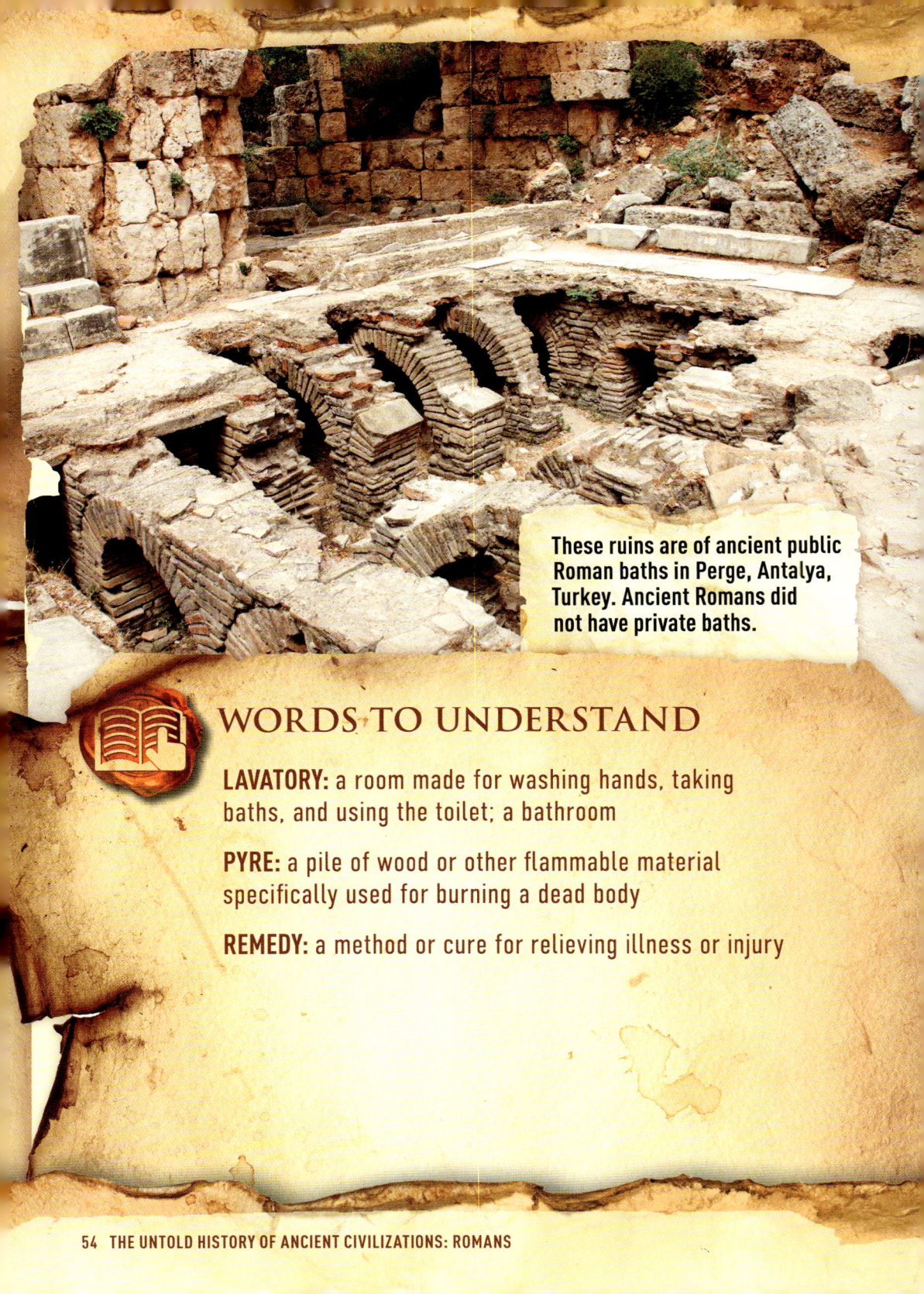

These ruins are of ancient public Roman baths in Perge, Antalya, Turkey. Ancient Romans did not have private baths.

WORDS TO UNDERSTAND

LAVATORY: a room made for washing hands, taking baths, and using the toilet; a bathroom

PYRE: a pile of wood or other flammable material specifically used for burning a dead body

REMEDY: a method or cure for relieving illness or injury

CHAPTER 11

THE ROMAN FITNESS PROGRAM

A long and happy life for a Roman tended to be a little more than half that today, about fifty years. Though many died in war, the main causes of death were childbirth, injuries, accidents, and infectious disease. Only one in four babies survived into childhood, and only half of the children lived to ten years old.

The Romans aimed to keep fit. The ideal was "a healthy mind in a healthy body." Men and boys were encouraged to exercise, and public baths and **lavatories** helped everyone keep clean.

There were many doctors in Roman towns. In fact, the Romans were the first to build hospitals. There were also wise women, midwives, and brutal army surgeons. None of them really understood the causes of disease, although they

Making coleslaw, an American cabbage dish, is super easy. Make sure to get an adult to help with the cooking.

CHAPTER 11: THE ROMAN FITNESS PROGRAM 55

CABBAGE CURES

Cabbage was one of the most popular plant remedies. It was crushed and spread on bruises and boils; stewed for headaches; fried in hot fat to treat sleeplessness; dried, powdered, and sniffed to clear blocked noses; and squeezed to extract juice to use as ear drops. (Do not try any of these.)

This Caduceus, the universal symbol of medicine, was discovered in ruins of Ephesus, Turkey.

could set bones and ease some aches and pains with massage and herbal medicines. But many of their **remedies** were dangerous, and few could cure serious illnesses. So Roman people also consulted witches for magic cures and prayed to the gods for help.

Funerals were important. They honored the dead, helped families cope with grief, and helped the dead person get to the underworld quickly. Dead bodies were not allowed to stay in cities and towns in case they spread disease. So, they were carried out in solemn processions, accompanied by mourners wearing wax face masks of ancestors. Then they were burned on a funeral **pyre** or buried alongside main roads in stone coffins known as *sarcophagi,* meaning "flesh eaters."

TEXT-DEPENDENT QUESTIONS

1. What was the average life expectancy of an ancient Roman?
2. What did the Romans use for a popular plant remedy?
3. Describe an ancient Roman funeral.

RESEARCH PROJECT

COLESLAW RECIPE

In ancient Rome, cabbage was popular and plentiful. It still is today, and it is used in making coleslaw, a typical American dish. With an adult's help, follow this recipe to create a delish and healthy coleslaw.

Ingredients:

- 1 cup (.24 L) light sour cream
- ½ cup (120 mL) mayonnaise
- ¼ cup (60 mL) white wine vinegar
- 2 tablespoons (29.57 mL) sugar
- 1 teaspoon (5 mL) salt
- ½ small green cabbage, shredded
- ½ small red cabbage, shredded
- 4 medium stalks celery, thinly sliced diagonally
- 2 medium carrots, coarsely grated

Directions:

1. In a bowl, mix together sour cream, mayonnaise, vinegar, sugar, and salt until thoroughly combined. Set aside.
2. In a large mixing bowl, combine the two cabbages, celery, and carrot. Add dressing and toss through. Cover and refrigerate for two hours or until chilled.

Notes:

* Buying pre-shredded cabbage makes this fast to prepare. A knife works, too, but make sure to ask an adult for help.

* Letting the salad sit makes it taste better.

* Don't worry if it turns pink. It's from the cabbage!

(Adapted from Kidspot.com)

ROMAN FACTS

Much of the Cloaca Maxima, built around 300 BC, still stands today.

FOUNDING FARMERS: According to legend, Romulus began to build Rome in 753 BC. But archaeologists think the city is even older. They have found the remains of farmers' huts dating from between 1000 and 800 BC. They think that these farmers, not Romulus or Remus, were probably the first citizens of Rome.

RIGHT NOT LEFT: Roman people thought that it was unlucky, or even wicked, to be left-handed. So, they kept babies' left arms tied closely to their bodies for the first few months of life. They hoped that this would teach them to use their right hand.

SEWER THING: The Romans built an elaborate network of drains and sewers under their city. The largest, called the Cloaca Maxima, built around 300 BC, was so big that a horse and cart could drive along inside it. It is still in use today.

PET LOVERS: The Romans were very fond of pets, especially dogs. They had many different breeds, including huge wolfhounds for hunting and small, white, fluffy Maltese terriers. They also kept tame fish and monkeys as well as pet birds, which they taught to talk.

ROAD BUILDERS: There were more than 53,000 miles (85 000 km) of roads throughout the Roman empire. The Romans first built roads so soldiers could march quickly to fight against rebels. Later, they were used by merchants, travelers, and government messengers who rode on fast horses.

LATIN SPEAKERS: The Romans spoke Latin. (Its name came from the region of Latium, in Italy.) Roman soldiers and government officials carried Latin all over the Roman Empire, and it became the language of scholars and the Roman Catholic Church for more than 1,000 years. Many modern European languages have developed from Latin, including Italian, Spanish, French, Romanian, and Portuguese.

SPECIAL DAYS: Romans liked birthday presents and held birthday parties. They also celebrated Mother's Day. But this was not much fun for the house owner's wife. She had to give all the women slaves the day off and do their work herself.

TOP MATERIAL: The Romans invented concrete and used it in many big buildings. It was cheaper and stronger than stone.

NATIONAL STADIUM: The Colosseum, opened in AD 80, was the largest amphitheater (public arena) in Rome. It was used to stage gladiator fights and mock sea battles. It could seat at least 50,000 people and had eighty separate entrances. Its walls were four tiers of stone and concrete arches. Cages for gladiators, prisoners, and wild animals were hidden under the floor. Spectators were sheltered by a huge, moveable canvas roof operated by men hauling on ropes. The surface of the arena was thickly covered with sand—to soak up all the blood.

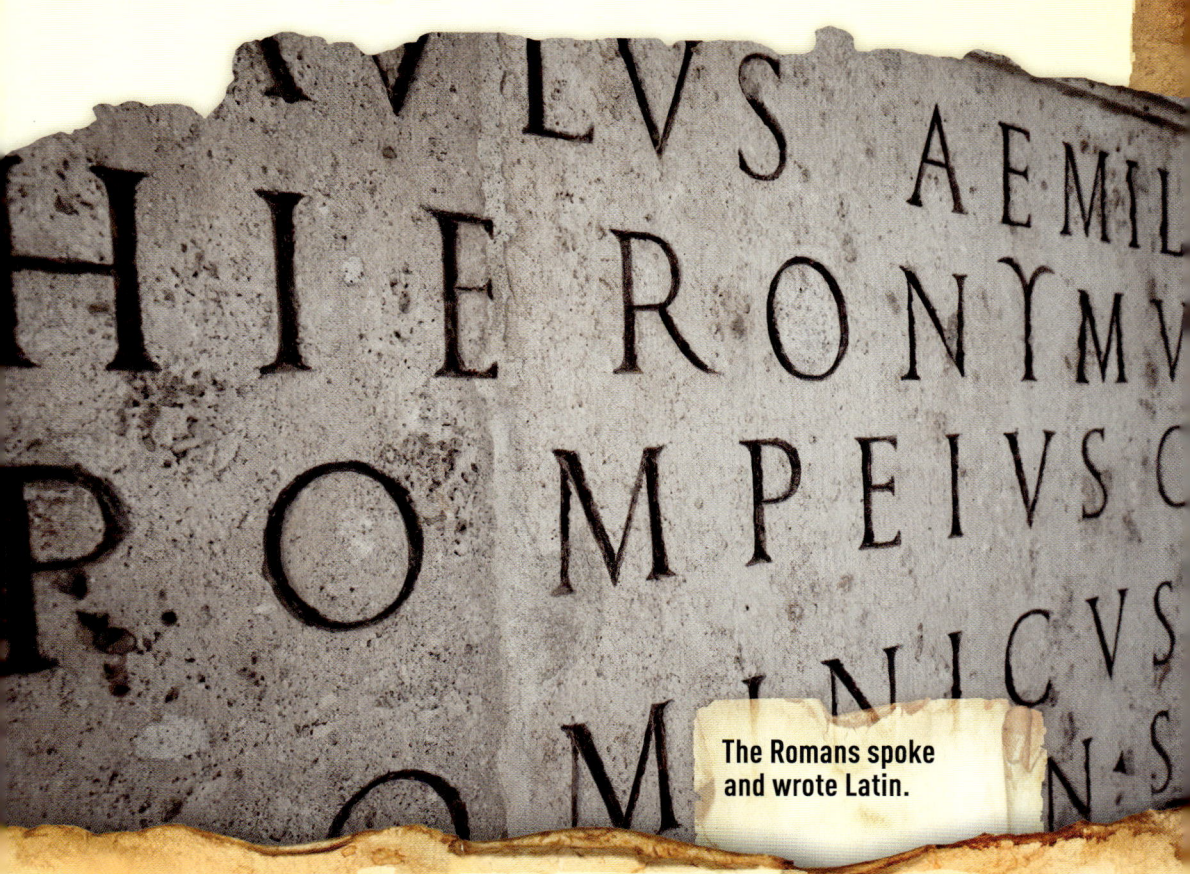

The Romans spoke and wrote Latin.

FURTHER RESOURCES

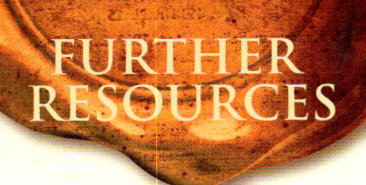

FURTHER READING

Cohn, Jessica. *The Ancient Romans*. New York: Gareth Stevens Publishing, 2013.

Macdonald, Fiona. *I Wonder Why Romans Wore Togas: and Other Questions about Rome*. New York: Kingfisher, 2012.

Mara, Wil. *The Romans*. New York: Marshall Cavendish Benchmark, 2012.

Williams, Marcia. *The Romans: Gods, Emperors, and Dormice*. Somerville, MA: Candlewick Press, 2013.

Woolf, Alex. *Meet the Ancient Romans*. New York: Gareth Stevens Publishing, 2015.

The Roman Colosseum is a massive structure that still hovers above Rome.

INTERNET RESOURCES

Surfing the Internet is the quickest way to find out information about the Romans. But the Internet is constantly changing, so if you can't find these Web sites, try searching using the word "Romans."

BBC
http://www.bbc.co.uk/schools/primaryhistory/romans/

Lots of facts, plus play a game where you get to be an archaeologist looking for Roman ruins.

HISTORY FOR KIDS
http://www.historyforkids.org/learn/romans/

Learn about all aspects of Roman life, plus find other great sources for even more information.

HANDS-ON HISTORY BBC
https://www.youtube.com/watch?v=D-VmbxpEFAA

Fun video on what it's like to be a Roman kid.

ANCIENT ROME FOR KIDS
http://www.rome.mrdonn.org/

Links to short articles about Roman life, plus a link to fun apps!

Roman soldiers had to be tough.

EDUCATIONAL VIDEO LINKS

Romans1: Learn about the rise of the Roman Empire in this video from *National Geographic*. http://x-qr.net/1Eik

Romans2: Do you wonder what it would be like living in ancient Rome? This video gives you a good idea of what it was like in a Roman family. http://x-qr.net/1Dnp

Romans3: Watch this video to learn how to make your own Roman toga. http://x-qr.net/1FXo

Romans4: Making coleslaw, an American cabbage dish, is super easy. Make sure to get an adult to help with the cooking. http://x-qr.net/1GD6

PHOTO CREDITS

Cover: © Cris Foto | Shutterstock, © WDG Photo | Shutterstock; Front Matter: © Vitaly Minko | Shutterstock; Chapter 1: © Vitaly Minko | Shutterstock, © Peter Hermes Furian | Shutterstock, © GoneWithTheWind | Shutterstock; Chapter 2: © Massan | Shutterstock, © Cris Foto | Shutterstock, © Shaun Jeffers | Shutterstock, © Cris Foto | Shutterstock; Chapter 3: © Inu | Shutterstock, © Klaus Hertz-Ladiges | Shutterstock, © mgallar | Shutterstock, © Brian Kinney | Shutterstock; Chapter 4: © Franco Volpato | Shutterstock, © pakpoom | Shutterstock, © Sandra Schramm | Shutterstock, © sonya etchison | Shutterstock, © burnel1 | Shutterstock; Chapter 5: © Mr.Piya Meena | Shutterstock, © Yulliii | Shutterstock, © Francesco Ricciardi Exp | Shutterstock, © Alex Alekseev | Shutterstock, © Peter Lorimer | Shutterstock; Chapter 6: © Fanfo | Shutterstock, © filippo giuliani | Shutterstock, © Igor Marusichenko | Shutterstock, © Peter Lorimer | Shutterstock, © Foodio | Shutterstock; Chapter 7: © Elliotte Rusty Harold |Shutterstock, © Cris Foto | Shutterstock, © Cris Fot | Shutterstock, © Peter Lorimer | Shutterstock, © Hein Nouwens | Shutterstock; Chapter 7: © antb | Shutterstock, © pajtica | Shutterstock, © Di Gregorio Giulio | Shutterstock, © David Gonzalez Rebollo | Shutterstock; Chapter 9: © joserpizarro | Shutterstock, © itechno | Shutterstock, © Kizel Cotiw-an | Shutterstock, © marcovarro | Shutterstock; Chapter 10: © zebra0209 | Shutterstock, © MinDof | Shutterstock, © Ververidis Vasilis | Shutterstock; Chapter 11: © Semjonow Juri | Shutterstock, © Hadrian | Shutterstock; Back Matter: © Lucamato | Shutterstock, 105764009 © taraki | Shutterstock, © InesVilasBoas | Shutterstock, © Zvonimir Atletic | Shutterstock; Back Cover: © Andrei Nekrassov | Shutterstock

INDEX

A
adoption, 26
Africans, 9
architecture, 6, 9, 14–15, 44, 58, 60
army, 50–53
Augustus, 13, 17, 27

B
baths, 42, 54
birthdays, 59
Byzantine Empire, 9

C
cabbage, 55–57, 62
    see also diet
Caligula, 13
Cato, 20
Celts, 9
children, 20, 24–26
Cicero, 12
circus, 42
Circus Maximus, 44
citizens, 6, 8, 50
Cloaca Maxima, 58
clothing, 20, 24, 36–40, 52
Colosseum, 59–60
Colosseum of Capua, 26
concrete, 59
consul, 10, 12
customs, 19–23, 26–27, 32–34, 38, 42–43, 48–49, 52, 54–56, 58–59

D
deities
    Diana, 48
    Janus, 48
    Juno, 48
    Jupiter, 46–47
    Mars, 47
    Mercury, 48
    Minerva, 39
    Mithras, 49
    Neptune, 48
    Sybele, 49
    Venus, 47
    Vesta, 47
    Vulcan, 48
Diana (deity), 48
dictator, 10, 12
diet, 16, 30–34, 55–57
divorce, 20
    see also family life; marriage
dogs, 58
domus, 14
    see also homes

E
education, 26–27
Egyptians, 9
emperor, 10, 12–13
entertainment, 42–44
equites, 6

F
family life, 19, 25, 62
farmers, 58

fire, 13, 17
funerals, 18, 56
    see also customs

G
games, 43
garum, 33
genii, 20
    see also deities; family life; gods; religion
geography, 7–8
Germans, 9
gladiators, 26, 42, 44–45, 59
Greeks, 9, 47
grooming, 23, 38

H
history, 7–9, 11–13, 38, 51, 58–59, 62
holidays, 43, 48–49, 59
homelessness, 16
homes, 14–17
Hortensius, 20

I
insulae, 16–17
    see also homes
Italians, 47

J
Janus (deity), 48
Jews, 9
Julius Caesar, 12
Juno (deity), 48
Jupiter (deity), 46–47

L

language, 59
lares, 20
   see also deities; family life; gods; religion
Latin, 59
laws, 7–8
legends, 8
life expectancy, 55

M

makeup, 38
map, 8
Marcus Aurelius, 10
marriage, 20–23
Mars (deity), 47
medical care, 54–56
Mercury (deity), 48
midwife, 24, 26, 55
Minerva (deity), 39
Mithras (deity), 49
murder, 11–12

N

naming customs, 26
   see also customs
Neptune (deity), 48
Nero, 13
noncitizens, 8, 50

P

palla, 36–37
   see also clothing
patricians, 8
pets, 58
plebeians, 8
Pluto (deity), 48
politics, 10–13, 20, 45
population, 9
porridge, 30–31
poverty, 28
priests, 47, 49
   see also religion

Q

QR Video
   make a Roman toga, 37, 62
   making coleslaw, 55, 62
   rise of the Roman Empire, 7, 62
   Roman family life, 19, 62

R

religion, 19, 46–48, 56
Remus, 8, 58
republic, 12
research project
   class distinctions, 17
   coleslaw recipe, 57
   Greek and Roman gods, 49
   Roman senate model, 13
   Roman soldier uniform, 53
   Roman toga, 41
   Roman toys and games, 45
   scavenger hunt, 9
   sweet-sour carrot recipe, 35
   tutulus braid, 22
   writing tablet, 29
Roman Catholic Church, 59
Roman Forum, 6
Romulus, 8, 58

S

sacrifices, 46, 48
   see also religion
Saturnalia, 49
Senate, 12–13
senators, 11
sewers, 58
slaves, 8–9, 17, 19, 26–27, 33, 45
soldiers, 50–52, 61
   see also army
spirits, 47
   see also religion
sports, 26, 42–43, 52
stola, 36–37
   see also clothing
Sybele (deity), 49

T

Tarquin the Proud, 11
taxes, 7
toga, 37

U

United States, 13

V

Venus (deity), 47
Vesta (deity), 47
villa, 14–15
   see also homes
Vulcan (deity), 48

W

war, 50
wax mask, 19
weapons, 51
weaving, 24, 27
witchcraft, 56
   see also medical care; religion
women, 20, 39
work, 43, 49, 58
writing, 28